THE TRY NOT TO LAUGH CHALLENGE

STOCKING STUFFER

— EDITION —

Try Not To Laugh Challenge
BONUS PLAY

Join our Joke Club and get the Bonus Play PDF!

Simply send us an email to:

TNTLPublishing@gmail.com

and you will get the following:

- 10 Hilarious, Bonus Jokes
- An entry in our **Monthly Giveaway** of a $50 Amazon Gift card!

We draw a new winner each month and will contact you via email!

Good luck!

😊

WELCOME TO THE
TRY NOT TO LAUGH CHALLENGE!

RULES OF THE GAME:

★ Grab a friend or family member, a pen/pencil, and your comedic skills! Determine who will be "Elf #1" and "Elf #2".

★ Take turns reading the jokes aloud to each other, and check the box next to each joke you get a laugh from! Each laugh box is worth 1 point, and the pages are labeled to instruct and guide when it is each player's turn.

★ Once you have both completed telling jokes in the round, tally up your laugh points and mark it down on each score page! There is a total of 10 Rounds.

★ Play as many rounds as you like! Once you reach the last round, Round 10, tally up ALL points from the previous rounds to determine who is the CHAMPION LAUGH MASTER!

★ Round 11 – The Tie-Breaker Round.

In the event of a tie, proceed to Round 11. This round will be 'Winner Takes All!', so whoever scores more laugh points in this round alone, is crowned the CHAMPION LAUGH MASTER!

TIP: Use an expressive voice, facial expressions, and even silly body movement to really get the most out of each joke and keep the crowd laughing!

Now, it's time to play!

ROUND

1

ELF 1

What singer was the best at decorating for Christmas?

A-WREATH-a Franklin!

☐ LAUGH

What does a wolf sing when he goes caroling?

"Deck the Howls."

☐ LAUGH

What do you call ten rockets on your feet?

Mistletoes!

☐ LAUGH

How did Santa Claus defeat the dragon?

He SLEIGH-ed it!

☐ LAUGH

ELF 1

Did you hear about the boy scout troop leader that accidentally took the boys tobogganing on a Black Diamond hill?

He really mis-SLED them!

○ LAUGH

Why did Santa retire and become a farmer?

He wanted to be a Jolly Rancher!

○ LAUGH

What do you call the fear of Santa?

CLAUS-trophobic!

○ LAUGH

What do you call a tasty wafer made of almonds?

Nutcracker!

○ LAUGH

Pass the book to Elf 2! →

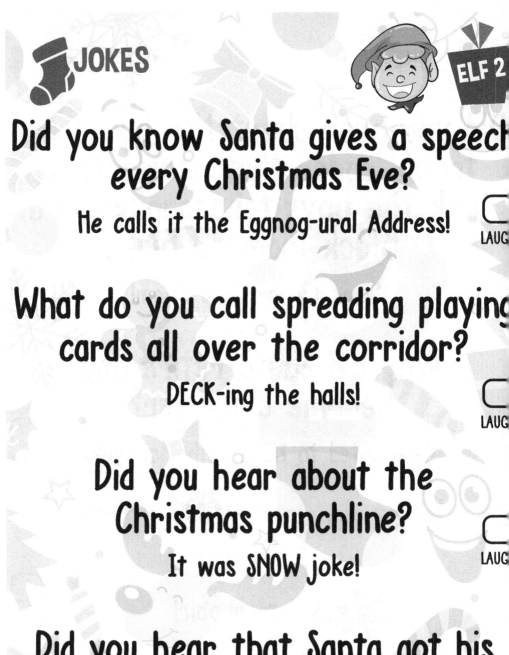

JOKES

ELF 2

Did you know Santa gives a speech every Christmas Eve?

He calls it the Eggnog-ural Address!

LAUGI

What do you call spreading playing cards all over the corridor?

DECK-ing the halls!

LAUGI

Did you hear about the Christmas punchline?

It was SNOW joke!

LAUGI

Did you hear that Santa got his leg joint replaced with a brick?

Now, he has a chim-KNEE!

LAUGI

 **JOKES**

How does the Christmas tree farmer feel about Christmas in the off-season?

He PINES for it!

 LAUGH

Is it better to advertise your Christmas tree company with a logo or catchy tune?

Jingle, all the way!

LAUGH

How will we track firewood sales?

YULE log them!

LAUGH

Mrs. Claus, what's the forecast for Christmas Eve?

"Rain, dear."

LAUGH

Time to add up your points! →

13

SCORE BOARD

Add up each Elf's laugh points for this round!

ELF 1 ___ /8
Total

ELF 2 ___ /8
Total

___
ROUND WINNER

ROUND 2

 **JOKES**

What did Saturn give Pluto for Christmas?

Five golden rings!

☐ LAUGH

What is a snowman's favorite breakfast?

Frosted Snowflakes!

☐ LAUGH

What is Santa's favorite cartoon channel?

NICK-elodeon!

☐ LAUGH

That snowman may look friendly, but believe me, he's s-NO-w angel!

☐ LAUGH

JOKES

ELF 1

What do you call two polar bears who cannot agree?

Polar opposites!

○ LAUGH

Where do you go when you want a Santa teddy bear?

Build-a-BEARD Workshop!

○ LAUGH

Did you hear one of Santa's reindeer has a new nephew?

She is excited to be an AUNT-ler! (Antler)

○ LAUGH

Which reindeer is the best at football?

Blitzen!

○ LAUGH

Pass the book to Elf 2! →

17

ELF 2

What does Mrs. Claus make when Santa is sick?

ELF-abet soup!

LAUG

What is a shark's favorite Christmas carol?

'We Fish You A Merry Christmas!'

LAUG

Why was Dasher eliminated from the Reindeer Games?

He was forced to WREATH-draw!

LAUG

What do the air fresheners in snowmen's houses smell like?

Carrots!

LAUG

Did you know Santa can square dance?

He once threw a HO-HO-Hoedown!

◻ LAUGH

What do puppies sing on Christmas?

"Up on the WOOF-top!"

◻ LAUGH

When does Santa wear socks?

When his mistle-TOES are cold!

◻ LAUGH

Why didn't the snowman get out of the way of the truck?

He was FROZEN in his tracks!

◻ LAUGH

Time to add up your points! →

SCORE BOARD

Add up each Elf's laugh points for this round!

ELF 1 ___/8
Total

ELF 2 ___/8
Total

_____
ROUND WINNER

ROUND

3

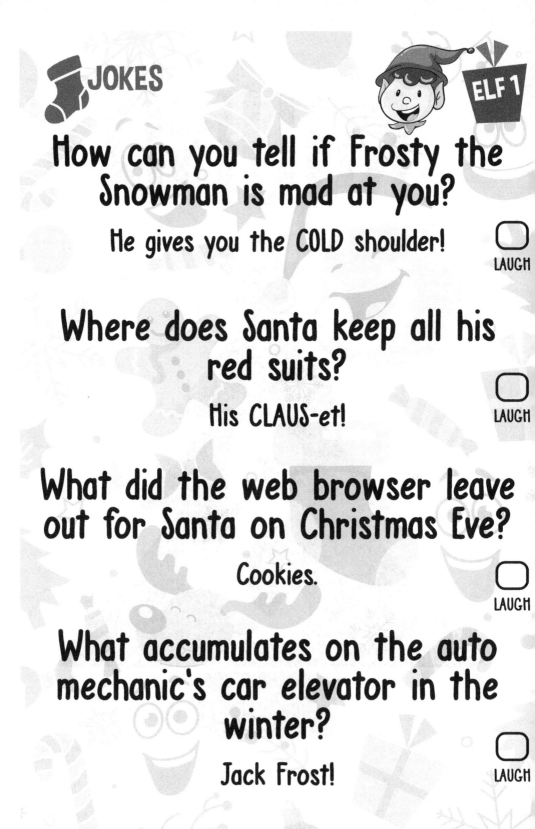

ELF 1

How can you tell if Frosty the Snowman is mad at you?

He gives you the COLD shoulder!

LAUGH

Where does Santa keep all his red suits?

His CLAUS-et!

LAUGH

What did the web browser leave out for Santa on Christmas Eve?

Cookies.

LAUGH

What accumulates on the auto mechanic's car elevator in the winter?

Jack Frost!

LAUGH

 **JOKES**

Which reindeer never says "Thank you"?

RUDE-olf!

☐ LAUGH

How do you wish a happy holiday to cheese?

"Season's GRATE-ings!"

☐ LAUGH

What do you call a doll you get on Christmas?

A Jolly Dolly!

☐ LAUGH

How does the monster feel after getting its nails clipped?

He misses claws! (Mrs. Claus)

☐ LAUGH

Pass the book to Elf 2! ➔

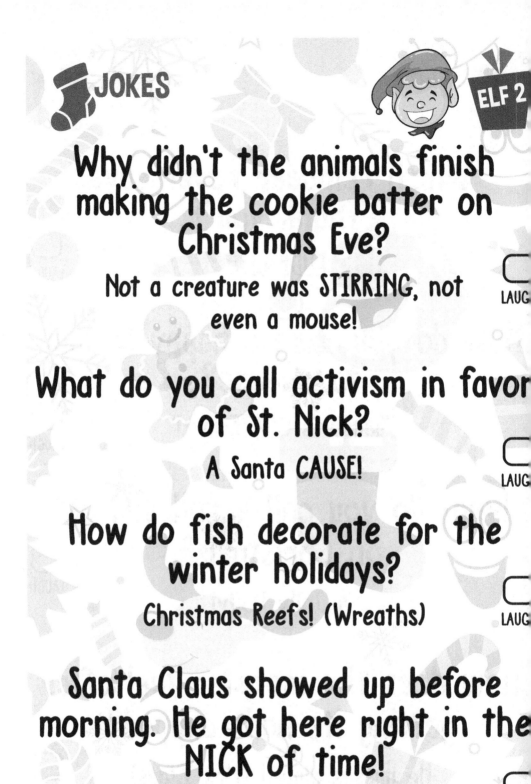

JOKES

ELF 2

Why didn't the animals finish making the cookie batter on Christmas Eve?

Not a creature was STIRRING, not even a mouse!

LAUG

What do you call activism in favor of St. Nick?

A Santa CAUSE!

LAUG

How do fish decorate for the winter holidays?

Christmas Reefs! (Wreaths)

LAUG

Santa Claus showed up before morning. He got here right in the NICK of time!

LAUG

 **JOKES**

 ELF 2

Why did the snowflakes gather together?

So they could have a snow-BALL!

LAUGH

Why are Santa's helpers so confident?

They have high ELF-esteem!

LAUGH

What do you hear when Santa gets a phone call mid-flight?

Sleigh bells ringing!

LAUGH

What is a horse's favorite part of Christmas?

The NEIGH-tivity scenes!

LAUGH

Time to add up your points! →

SCORE BOARD

Add up each Elf's laugh points for this round!

ELF 1   /8
_____
Total

ELF 2   /8
_____
Total

_____
ROUND WINNER

ROUND

 JOKES

 ELF 1

What is Santa's favorite '70s song?

Bohemian WRAP-sody.

☐ LAUGH

How does Santa's helper direct the sleigh route?

He POINSETTIA map to show the next stop!

☐ LAUGH

What's the slogan for non-dairy eggnog?

"Soy to the world!"

☐ LAUGH

What do you write in a holiday card to a cow?

"Dairy Christmas!"

☐ LAUGH

 **JOKES**

What do you call Santa's smallest dog?

Santa's Little Yelper!

☐ LAUGH

What do sea urchins sing for Christmas?

Christmas Corals!

☐ LAUGH

Why did the snowman melt when he won the lottery?

He suddenly became very LIQUID!

 ☐ LAUGH

How does a snowman stop eating meat?

Cold turkey!

☐ LAUGH

Pass the book to Elf 2! →

What do elves listen to in Santa's workshop?

Wrap music!

LAUG

Who always gets first place at the North Pole game nights?

The Peng-WINS!

LAUG

Where does a mistletoe go, when it becomes a movie star?

HOLLY-wood!

LAUG

I saw you eat one of my Christmas cookies... YULE be sorry!

LAUG

 JOKES

 ELF 2

Did you hear what Rudolph did to the bullies?

Let's just say they USED to laugh and call him names!

☐ LAUGH

What do Italian elves make on Christmas?

Chicken ELF-redo!

☐ LAUGH

Who is best at detecting when Santa's helpers are around?

Someone with high ELF-awareness!

☐ LAUGH

Where does Santa stay when he is far from the North Pole?

A Ho-Ho-Hotel!

☐ LAUGH

Time to add up your points! →

31

SCORE BOARD

Add up each Elf's laugh points for this round!

ELF 1   /8
Total

ELF 2   /8
Total

ROUND WINNER

ROUND

5

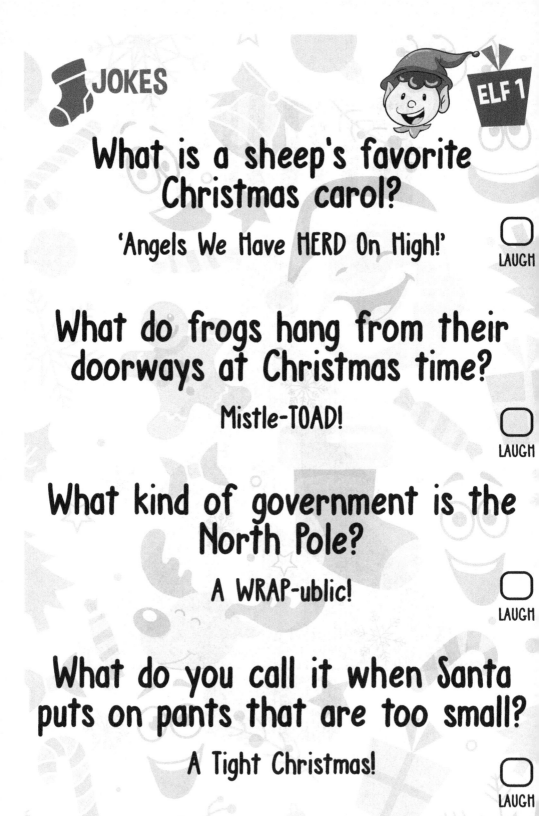

JOKES

ELF 1

What is a sheep's favorite Christmas carol?

'Angels We Have HERD On High!'

LAUGH

What do frogs hang from their doorways at Christmas time?

Mistle-TOAD!

LAUGH

What kind of government is the North Pole?

A WRAP-ublic!

LAUGH

What do you call it when Santa puts on pants that are too small?

A Tight Christmas!

LAUGH

ELF 1

Why did the penguin quit his job?

Honestly, it's SNOW-body's business!

☐ LAUGH

What is it called if Santa gets donuts instead of cookies?

A HOLE-y Night!

☐ LAUGH

What does Santa dress the reindeer as for Halloween?

Cari-BOO!

☐ LAUGH

What do the reindeer do when they are frustrated?

They ad-VENT to each other!

☐ LAUGH

Pass the book to Elf 2! ➡

ELF 2

What do fish wear on Christmas?

Ugly Christmas WET-ters!

LAUG.

Why do people say Santa is very zen?

He has a calm PRESENTS about him!

LAUG.

Bright white all around, and still, I'm hard to see. Make sure you don't catch a cold, when you get caught by me! What am I?

A Blizzard.

LAUG.

Who delivers crabs' presents on Christmas Eve?

Sandy Claws!

LAUG.

 **JOKES**

What do elves do in the summertime to relax?

Hang out by the snowf-LAKE!

☐ LAUGH

What does a snowman get when he trims his beard?

Shaved Ice!

☐ LAUGH

What did the hipster candle say to the match?

It's about to be candle-LIT, fam!

☐ LAUGH

Who does Santa hire for catering?

Christmas COOK-ies!

☐ LAUGH

Time to add up your points! →

SCORE BOARD

Add up each Elf's laugh points for this round!

ELF 1   /8
         _____
            Total

ELF 2   /8
         _____
            Total

_____

ROUND WINNER

ROUND

6

 **JOKES**

What do sheep say on Christmas?

"FLEECE Navidad!"

○ LAUGH

Giving is better than receiving. I 100 PRESENT agree with you!

○ LAUGH

What does Mrs. Claus do when she is mad at Santa?

She gives him the COAL shoulder!

○ LAUGH

What does Santa say before he takes a photo?

"Sleigh cheese!"

○ LAUGH

 **JOKES**

 **ELF 1**

What do you call Santa's legs when he puts on tights?

Stocking Stuffers!

☐ LAUGH

How would you describe Santa in his suit, when he is feeling sad?

Patriotic. – Red, white, and blue!

☐ LAUGH

What do Santa's helpers post to Instagram?

Elfies! (Selfies)

☐ LAUGH

Why do carolers not like to give people a heads up that they are coming by?

☐ LAUGH

There's NOEL-ement of surprise!

Pass the book to Elf 2! ➡

JOKES

Did you hear about how Santa is OCD?

He's making a list, then he's checking it over, and over, and over AGAIN.

☐ LAUGH

Who was the first reindeer in space?

Comet!

☐ LAUGH

What comes after a "N Christmas Tree?"

"O Christmas Tree!"

 ☐ LAUGH

What do you call an eccentric piece of frozen rain?

Snowflake!

☐ LAUGH

 **JOKES**

ELF 2

Why don't snowmen get angry?
They don't want to have a meltdown!

LAUGH

What does McDonald's serve at the North Pole?
Iceberg-ers!

LAUGH

What is a pair of reindeer worth?
2 bucks!

LAUGH

It's a family secret that no one really likes grandma's figgy pudding. We are just PUDDING up with it to not hurt her feelings!

LAUGH

Time to add up your points! →

43

SCORE BOARD

Add up each Elf's laugh points for this round!

ELF 1   /8
Total

ELF 2   /8
Total

ROUND WINNER

ROUND

 **JOKES**

 **ELF 1**

What do elves say if they don't like their food?

"Snow, thank you."

☐ LAUGH

How does Santa take his photos?

With a North Pole-aroid!

☐ LAUGH

What is a chicken's favorite Christmas food?

EGGnog!

☐ LAUGH

What do you call people who slide on ice barefoot?

Cheap-skates!

☐ LAUGH

JOKES

What is Rudolph's favorite pastime?

He always has his nose in a book.
They say he's very well-RED!

☐ LAUGH

What is a crocodile's favorite holiday tune?

"CROC-ing Around the Christmas Tree!"

☐ LAUGH

What does Jack Frost do when he needs a ride?

He HAILS a cab!

☐ LAUGH

What do you call Santa's cat?

Santa's CLAWS!

☐ LAUGH

Pass the book to Elf 2! ➜

47

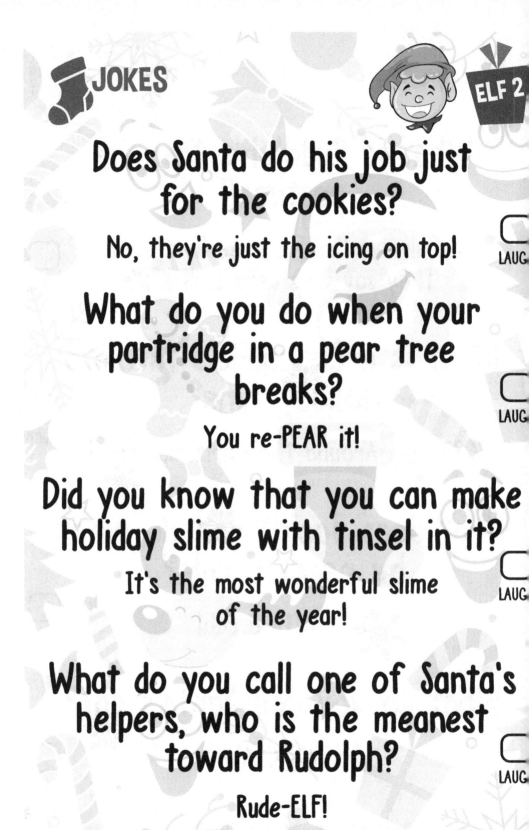

JOKES

ELF 2

Does Santa do his job just for the cookies?

No, they're just the icing on top!

LAUG

What do you do when your partridge in a pear tree breaks?

You re-PEAR it!

LAUG

Did you know that you can make holiday slime with tinsel in it?

It's the most wonderful slime of the year!

LAUG

What do you call one of Santa's helpers, who is the meanest toward Rudolph?

Rude-ELF!

LAUG

 JOKES

Have you ever seen an angry snowman?

Of course not, they're all pretty CHILL!

☐ LAUGH

What do you call it when Santa cuts himself shaving?

Nick!

☐ LAUGH

What do you call Rudolph when he has read too many detective stories?

☐ LAUGH

Rudolph the Caught You Red-Handed Reindeer!

What do you call a snowman on broadway?

Frosty the SHOWman!

☐ LAUGH

Time to add up your points! →

49

SCORE BOARD

Add up each Elf's laugh points for this round!

ELF 1   /8
            _____
            Total

ELF 2   /8
            _____
            Total

ROUND WINNER

ROUND

8

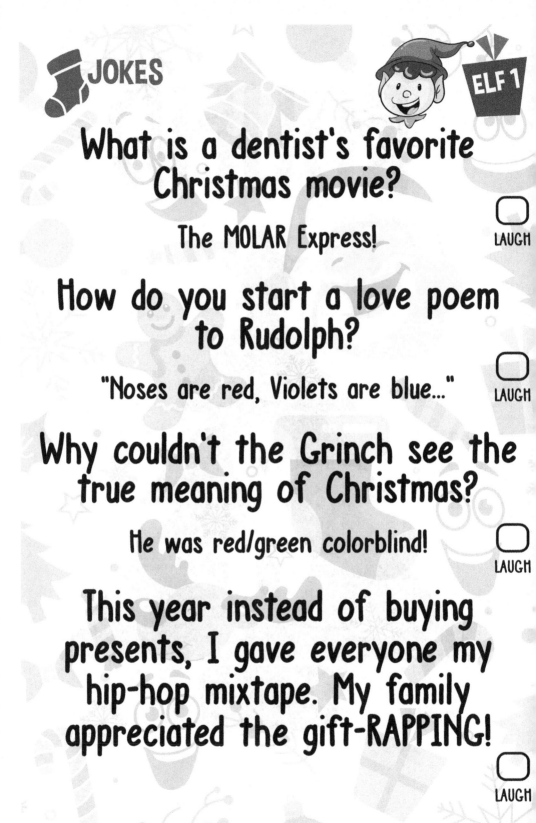

ELF 1

What is a dentist's favorite Christmas movie?

The MOLAR Express!

○ LAUGH

How do you start a love poem to Rudolph?

"Noses are red, Violets are blue..."

○ LAUGH

Why couldn't the Grinch see the true meaning of Christmas?

He was red/green colorblind!

○ LAUGH

This year instead of buying presents, I gave everyone my hip-hop mixtape. My family appreciated the gift-RAPPING!

○ LAUGH

 JOKES

Why do snowmen avoid cuteness?

It melts their hearts!

☐ LAUGH

What does Santa do in the summer?

He goes on SLEIGH-cation!

☐ LAUGH

What are Santa's favorite types of bears?

North Pole-ar bears.

☐ LAUGH

Why was the class so let down?

Santa gave them PRESENT-ations for Christmas!

☐ LAUGH

Pass the book to Elf 2! ➔

 **JOKES**

ELF 2

What do you call a naughty boy?
Cole! (Coal)

LAUG

Why did the grizzly buy snowshoes?
To put on his BEAR feet!

LAUG

Why couldn't the eskimo pay his bills?
His accounts were FROZEN!

LAUG

What do you call a basketball team of Santas?
The Nicks!

LAUG

ELF 2

Why do hip-hop artists love Christmas?

Because of all the wrapping!

☐ LAUGH

Why did Santa give the shoelace coal?

He was on the KNOTTY list!

☐ LAUGH

Who appears if you lose one of your gifts?

The Ghost of Christmas Presents!

☐ LAUGH

Why did the chess club go to the shooting range to brag about their competition wins?

'Tis the season for chess nuts boasting while they open fire!

☐ LAUGH

Time to add up your points! →

SCORE BOARD

Add up each Elf's laugh points for this round!

ELF 1   /8
Total

ELF 2   /8
Total

ROUND WINNER

ROUND

9

 JOKES

 ELF 1

Where in the bookstore do Santa's helpers go to improve?

The ELF-help section!

☐ LAUGH

How can you recognize Santa?

YULE know him, when you see him!

☐ LAUGH

What is the snowman's favorite beverage?

Frost-tea!

☐ LAUGH

What do you call a stone that plays Christmas music?

Jingle Bell ROCK!

☐ LAUGH

JOKES

ELF 1

What do you call a wet doe?

RAIN-deer!

☐ LAUGH

What do you call it when Santa surveys his elves?

A North Poll!

☐ LAUGH

What do you call a medieval warrior made of Swiss cheese?

A HOLE-y knight!

☐ LAUGH

What does basil write in its Christmas cards?

"Seasoning's Greetings!"

☐ LAUGH

Pass the book to Elf 2! →

ELF 2

I drew a graph of my favorite holiday desserts. It's a PIE chart!

LAUG

What happened to the mischievous puppy that chewed up Santa's boots?

LAUG

He was put on the GNAW-ty list!

Why is Christmas Eve the best time to meditate?

LAUG

Because your mind is so focused on the PRESENT!

The fish asked his mom why his Christmas stocking was full of shells and sand. She replied, "Tis the sea, son."

LAUG

JOKES

What does a stocking say when you offer it dessert?

"No thanks, I'm already STUFFED!"

LAUGH

Why do bananas make good presents?

They're already wrapped!

LAUGH

What do you call a rabid male made out of ice?

FROTHY the Snowman!

LAUGH

When is it the present moment in winter?

S'now!

LAUGH

Time to add up your points! →

SCORE BOARD

Add up each Elf's laugh points for this round!

ELF 1 _____ **/8**
Total

ELF 2 _____ **/8**
Total

_____
ROUND WINNER

ROUND

10

 **JOKES**

 ELF 1

How do you keep a Christmas tree warm?

A FIR coat!

○ LAUGH

How does Frosty the Snowman introduce himself?

"I'm Frosty, ICE to meet you!"

○ LAUGH

What do you call a goat sliding down a mountain?

Alpine skiing!

○ LAUGH

Who led the French in the invasion of the North Pole?

Joan of Arctic!

○ LAUGH

 **JOKES**

What's Santa's elves favorite car?

TOY-ota.

☐ LAUGH

What does the bamboo do on Christmas?

Watch out for Panda Claws!

☐ LAUGH

What do you call a medieval soldier, who doesn't talk much?

A Silent Knight!

☐ LAUGH

What do you call it when winter and summer acknowledge each other?

"Season's Greetings!"

☐ LAUGH

Pass the book to Elf 2! ➞

65

 **JOKES**

 ELF 2

What can a hyphen be found doing in winter?

DASH-ing through the snow!

◻ LAUG

What hangs over Santa's porch?

A Christmas Eave!

◻ LAUG

What is a squid's favorite Christmas carol?

J-INK-le Bells!

◻ LAUG

Don't hold it against me when I grab you by the throat. To keep you against me, and help out your coat. What am I?

A Scarf!

◻ LAUG

 **JOKES**

What made the snowman naughty?

He was SLED astray.

☐ LAUGH

How do you get permission to leave class, to put up wreaths on lockers?

☐ LAUGH

You ask your teacher for a HOLLY-pass!

How did Dasher misspell Rudolph's name?

He thought there was NOEL before the "P." (No L)

☐ LAUGH

What does a mommy snowman sing to put her little snowman to sleep?

'Ice Ice, Baby!'

☐ LAUGH

Time to add up your points! →

SCORE BOARD

Add up each Elf's laugh points for this round!

ELF 1   /8
_____
Total

ELF 2   /8
_____
Total

_____
ROUND WINNER

Add up all your points from each round. The ELF with the most points is crowned
The Laugh Master!
In the event of a tie, continue to Round 11 - The Tie-Breaker Round!

ELF 1

_____
Grand Total

ELF 2

_____
Grand Total

_____
THE LAUGH MASTER

ROUND

11

TIE-BREAKER
(Winner Takes ALL!)

 **JOKES**

 ELF 1

What do little crabs like best about Christmas?

Sandy Claws!

LAUG

How does the frog princess find her prince on Christmas?

Under the mistle-TOAD!

LAUG

What did Santa use when he broke his leg going down the chimney?

A candy cane!

LAUG

If a snow-covered holiday is a "White Christmas," what do you call Christmas at the beach?

Yule-TIDE!

LAUG

JOKES

ELF 1

What did peanut butter write on its Christmas cards?

"Have a JELLY Christmas!"

☐ LAUGH

How long can a Christmas tree stay up?

FIR-ever!

☐ LAUGH

What do elk write on their Christmas cards?

"Merry Christ-MOOSE!"

☐ LAUGH

Why do lumberjacks get good posture from holding up trees?

It's good LUMBAR support!

☐ LAUGH

Pass the book to Elf 2! →

 **JOKES**

 **ELF 2**

What do you call it when a snowman crashes on a ski jump?

Ice cream!

LAUG

Which vegetable can sink the Titanic?

ICEBERG lettuce!

LAUG

Why do snowmen make good telemarketers?

They like COLD calling!

LAUG

What is an elf's favorite toothpaste flavor?

Orna-MINT!

 LAUG

ELF 2

Which Christmas carol was written in medieval times?

Silent Knight!

O LAUGH

What do you become if you get upset on Christmas?

Navi-MAD!

O LAUGH

What is the difference between a bowl of pears and polar bears?

You can eat the pears, but the polar bears can eat you!

O LAUGH

What do you call it when a snowman looks at Medusa and melts?

Hydration!

O LAUGH

Time to add up your points! ➔

Add up all your points from the Tie-Breaker Round.
The Elf with the most points is crowned
The Laugh Master!

ELF 1 /8 Total

ELF 2 /8 Total

THE LAUGH MASTER

Check out our

Visit our Amazon Store at:

other joke books!

Made in the USA
Coppell, TX
20 December 2020